Nichiren's Nationalism: A Buddhist Rhetoric of a Shinto Teaching

by
Achilles S.C. Gacis

ISBN: 1-58112-110-5

DISSERTATION.COM

USA • 2000

Nichiren's Nationalism: A Buddhist Rhetoric of a Shinto Teaching

Dissertation.com
USA • 2000

ISBN: 1-58112-110-5

www.dissertation.com/library/1121105a.htm

NICHIREN'S NATIONALISM:

A BUDDHIST RHETORIC OF A SHINTO TEACHING

A THESIS SUBMITTED TO THE GRADUATE DIVISION OF THE
UNIVERSITY OF HAWAII IN PARTIAL FULFILLMENT OF THE
REQUIREMENTS FOR THE DEGREE OF

MASTER OF ARTS

IN

RELIGION

AUGUST 1992

BY

Achilles S.C. Gacis

Thesis Committee:

George Tanabe, Chairman
David Chappell
Anatole Lyovin

TABLE OF CONTENTS

At this time the heavenly deities, all with one command, said to the two deities Izanagi-nö-Mikötö and Izanami-nö-Mikötö: "Complete and solidify this drifting land!" Giving them the Heavenly Jeweled Spear, they entrusted the mission to them. Thereupon, the two deities stood on the Heavenly Floating Bridge and lowering the jeweled spear, stirred with it. They stirred the brine with a churning-churning sound; and when they lifted up [the spear] again, the brine dripping down from the tip of the spear piled up and became an island.

-Kojiki, Book One, Chapter Three.

PREFACE

The cosmogonic mythology of Japan has provided a divine
ethno-spiritual nationalism for its inhabitants since its
inception. In the introduction to his translated work of the
Kojiki, Donald L. Philippi writes:

> Very often the beginnings of a nation's history involve
> tensions, contradictions, and difficulties which
> continue to operate, overtly or latently, for many
> centuries. Even if the external forms of life undergo
> change-even revolutionary change-many of the early
> concepts, attitudes, and beliefs maintain a surprising
> vitality, influencing the nation throughout its entire
> history.[1]

The influence of Shintō religion permeated Japanese society from
the agricultural classes to the aristocracy. Shintō provided a
spiritual nationalism and ethno-centricity for the Japanese that
not only affirmed the divine lineage of the Emperor back to the
sun-goddess, but also the divinity of the land/the nation as
being the abode of the kami (deities). This type of "spiritual
habitation" of the country meant that proper religious
observances had to be kept in order to appease the kami and
guarantee a peaceful and fruitful relationship between the nation
and the gods.

This concept for maintaining the security and prosperity of
the nation by following correct spiritual practices was kept
right up to the early Kamakura period when Buddhism was in a
process of reformation. This was due in part to the troubled
atmosphere of the time. War, famine, pestilence, religious

---

[1] Donald L. Philippi, Trans. Kojiki (Tokyo: University of
Tokyo Press, 1968), p. 3.

institutional corruption, these matters were of prime importance because their deteriorating nature attacked the very foundation of Japanese culture, identity, and all that was deemed sacred for the security and stability of the nation. For some leaders of Buddhist movements in the early Kamakura period, nationalism was either of secondary importance or not to be addressed at all. But for Nichiren, considered by his followers as a Buddhist saint and prophet, the importance of nationalism was a strong concept given the historical circumstances of his time.

Regarding the unfortunate natural and societal situation of Japan in the early Kamakura period, Nichiren asked the basic question of "why is this going on?" He attempted to answer this question by delving into the scriptures of established Buddhist sects and utilizing their various insights to validate his unique answer(s) to the nation's plight. Trained as he was in the Tendai Buddhist sect, Nichiren's vocabulary was rich with Buddhist terminology, and his nationalistic propagation and analogies for validating his point had strong yet covert Shintō characteristics. It was because of the fusion of Buddhist salvific teaching and divine Shintō nationalism that Nichiren gave primacy to the concerns of the country during a time of national crises.

A Summary of Contents

Chapter One, "Religion and Nationalism in Early Kamakura Society" introduces the issues that affected the nation in the early Kamakura period. The first section points out the historical background of the time that was considered to be a spiritually significant age according to Buddhist chronology. The next section on the "Religious Answers to National Problems" provides a prelude to how the indigenous religious tradition of Shintō attempted to define its leaders and their right to rule as well as the divine protection that was to be given them by the native deities. The imported Buddhist teachings provided a new perspective to the national problems through an examination of existing conditions as possibly being consequences of immoral acts. The various characteristics of the teachings of the most prominent Buddhist leaders of the early Kamakura period are introduced in the next section of "Buddhism: Kamakura's Five Reformers." In the following four sections ("Hōnen," "Eisai," "Shinran," and "Dōgen"), a few specifics on the differences and similarities of the nationalistic perspectives of the first four Buddhist reformers are examined.

Chapter Two, "Nichiren," looks at the particulars in the fifth reformer's life that can help to clarify his approach toward providing a viable solution for the nation's problems. This is done by examining his life as being the product of "A Buddhist-Shintō Fusion." In this chapter I argue that Nichiren's upbringing and lifelong exposure to the indigenous tradition of Shintō (which emphasized the divine nature of Japan) provided an ethno-spiritual nationalistic element to his Buddhist teaching (which stressed complete faith in his interpretation of the message and meaning of the _Lotus Sūtra_).

Chapter Three surveys the "Nationalism in Nichiren's Writings" by examining the methodology that Nichiren used in propagating his teachings. One of his principles for conversion was _shakubuku_, which he supported by referring to scripture. His political aspirations through the use of religion are examined in the next section. Nichiren's affirmation of Shintō is presented in a comparison and contrast of his Budddhist teachings to his Shintō activities. Finally, I conclude with some reflection on how Nichiren was primarily a Shintō influenced nationalist who supported his views with Buddhist teaching and how this imported religion (Buddhism) was made Japanese by its interdigitation with Shintō.

CHAPTER I

RELIGION AND NATIONALISM IN EARLY KAMAKURA SOCIETY

The shift from the Heian (800-1200) to the Kamakura period (1186-1333) marked a turbulent era in Japanese medieval history. The religious atmosphere of the time concerned itself with a number of issues. Why were plagues and wars so prevalent? What did the troubled times mean for a divine nation like Japan that was inhabited by kami (deities)? Why were the hierarchs of both church and state so preoccupied with scandal, corruption, and intrigue? According to Japanese historian Masaharu Anesaki:

> It was not a mere political revolution, but social, moral, and religious at the same time. The Buddhist hierarchies lost their prestige to a large extent, together with their political supporters at court, ceremonies and mysteries were much discredited, while undercurrents of unrest and aspiration manifested themselves in various ways.[2]

The unrest felt by the common class was expressed through their religion. Folk practices that were a fusion of indigenous Shintō beliefs and Buddhist salvific rituals became the means by which the commoners might find some explanation for national problems as well as spiritual solace and material relief.

In order to better understand how the medieval Japanese used religion to address their national (and ultimately personal) concerns, the following items will be explored: the historical background of the Kamakura period, proposed religious answers,

---

[2] Masaharu Anesaki, <u>History of Japanese Religion</u>, (London: Kegan Paul, Trench, Trubner and Co. Ltd., 1930) p. 167.

1

the response by the indigenous Shintō system (along with its relation to Buddhism) and finally what prominent Buddhist reformers had to say regarding the national problems that confronted Kamakura Japan.

Historical Background

The Japanese medieval period began near the end of the twelfth century and lasted through the sixteenth century. Japan's first great military ruler, Minamoto Yoritomo, rose to power in 1192 and established a powerful feudal regime (bakufu) at Kamakura near present day Tokyo.[3] This marked the beginning of the Kamakura period which lasted until 1333. As to why Japan's early medieval period was filled with military feudalism, one needs to look at two elements that contributed to the shift from the previous high-cultured and aristocratic Heian period to the turbulent Kamakura period.

The first is a corruption of the elitist aristocracy that gradually failed to address the basic issues and needs of the nation as time progressed. According to Kitagawa:

> However, a radical event, such as the establishment of the feudal regime, was not possible unless there was a general feeling of approval on the part of the people toward the necessary correction of what was basically wrong with the previous government.[4]

---

[3] Joseph M. Kitagawa, Religion in Japanese History (New York: Columbia University Press, 1966), p. 86.

[4] Ibid., 87.

What appeared to be "wrong" was the widening gap between the commoners and the guardians and teachers of culture, religion, and the socio-economic/political stratum. Kitagawa further explains:

> In a definite way, the Kamakura period was marked by the rejection of artificial culture delicately concocted by courtiers and clergy, in favor of a more natural spirit and indigenous forms of culture and society.[5]

The desire for the "indigenous forms of culture and society" was based on the aristocracy's overemphasis on the propagation of Chinese governmental structure and culture as being superior to the Japanese. However important the cultural and political revolution of the Kamakura period was for the economic good of the common citizen, it was the radicalization of religious teaching that provided a spiritual base for the masses, who desired an improved condition of their lives. Though change occurred, it did not improve society on the whole. Change took place, and the crisis of the times was reflected in the claim by many Buddhists that this was the arrival of a spiritually significant time period in Buddhist teaching: mappō, the age of the final dharma.

This brings up the second element in the overall shift from the Heian to the Kamakura periods. What was strongly viewed as a spiritual matter were the natural disasters of earthquakes and plagues that afflicted the populace all too frequently. This is not to say that governmental corruption and incompetency were

---

[5] Ibid., p. 8.

3

viewed as mere human problems unaffected or uninfluenced by spiritual matters. It was a fraction of the multi-faceted problems that Buddhism claimed would arise as the generations passed further and further away from the age of Shakyamuni's original teachings. As Stone points out:

> Sūtras and treatises divide this process of degeneration into three sequential periods beginning from the time of the Buddha's death: the age of the True Dharma (Skt. Saddharma, Jap. Shōbō) the age of the Counterfeit Dharma (Saddharma-pratirūpaka, Zōhō) and the age of the Final Dharma (saddharma-vipralopa, Mappō).[6]

One way of interpreting Japan's natural and societal problems that was within the scope of the people was with a spiritual perspective. Aside from the native/internal problems that affected the social stability of Japan, an external problem arose in the form of the Mongol invasion of Chinese and Korean troops in 1274. This invasion contributed to heavy losses for the Japanese, who were now convinced that the age of mappō was indeed the cause of the frequent calamities that befell their country.

Religious Answers to National Problems

With the onslaught of national calamities, the cause of which was understood through a Buddhist teaching (mappō), it seemed only natural that the existing dialogue between the clerics controlling the major temples and the governmental

---

[6] Jackie Stone, "Seeking Enlightenment in the Last Age: Mappo Thought in Kamakura Buddhism." Part 1, The Eastern Buddhist Vol. 18, No. 1 (Spring, 1985; Kyoto: The Eastern Buddhist Society) p. 29.

4

aristocrats controlling the structure of society would strengthen. The urgency of proper spiritual practice for the good of the nation took precedence over other mundane matters. If the world (Japan) drifted away from the original teaching of Shakyamuni, and the age of mappō was upon the country, then perhaps a return to the original teaching of the Buddha would assure spiritual peace and perhaps worldly prosperity for all. It is precisely at this point of national crisis that new religious leaders arose and "religion" stepped forward and boldly proclaimed to have the panacea for the country's ailments. An interesting aspect of this national spiritual therapy was that a number of practices were propagated as the solutions to the existing and widespread problems.

Though these propagations were Buddhist practices, they were not free from religious and political elements found in the teachings of the indigenous Shintō religion, which emphasized divine ethno-spiritual nationalism. For most Buddhist leaders, Shintō provided the basic religious means of explaining things such as one's divine right to rule, how natural phenomena affect man as well as can be affected by man, and how a country can perceive itself as being the abode of nation protecting deities.

Shintō

With the death of the boy-Emperor Antoku (1178-1185) at the hands of the Minamoto clan, questions arose concerning the Imperial family's divine lineage. What enabled the Kamakura

shogunate to overshadow the Imperial family's hereditary, divine
right to rule? Why did the Imperial family's tutelary deities
not defend the boy Emperor? These and other questions were
important because of the strong relationship Shintō had with the
Imperial family and the nation. Allan G. Grapard described the
relationship between Shintō and Japanese nationalism:

> Shintō may be looked at as a multiheaded phenomenon:
> appearing at times as a loosely structured set of
> practices, creeds, and attitudes rooted in local
> communities, it is also a strictly defined and
> organized religion at the level of the state.[7]

Hirai defined Shintō as:

> The traditional indigenous religious practices of the
> Japanese people as well as their worldview, based on
> their concept of kami. Shintō is a "national
> religion," practiced for the most part by Japanese
> (including overseas immigrants), and which, with the
> exception of several sects, has no founder but instead
> developed naturally.[8]

This "national religion" was practiced by the Japanese
because of their understanding of what kami can do for the
country. One of the kami's duties was to provide divine
protection for the nation they inhabit (Japan) and to provide
protection to one of their descendants, the Emperor.

The Emperor claimed to be a descendant of the Sun Goddess
Amaterasu-Omi-Kami. According to Japanese mythology, the
Imperial family's lineal descent from Amaterasu was established

---

[7] Allan G. Grapard, "Shinto" in Kodansha Encyclopedia of
Japan, (Tokyo: Harper and Row, 1983) v.7, p. 125.

[8] Naofusa Hirai, "Shinto" in The Encyclopedia of Religion,
Mircea Eliade, ed. (New York: MacMillan,1987)
v.13, p. 280.

through her grandson Ninigi-nö-Mikötö, who descended to the earth
to rule the islands of Japan. The loyalty that an individual
would show to the Imperial throne and the veneration of Amaterasu
was one and the same thing. Holtom writes:

> The emperor, ruling in a line that reaches back
> unbroken to her historically manifested person, is the
> extension in time and space of her very body and soul.
> The god-emperor and the great deity mediate one and the
> same will. Reverence for one is reverence for the
> other. To fail to honor the sun-goddess is to fail in
> the first duty of a subject to the state; it is treason
> against the sacred national structure itself.[9]

The early Japanese did not draw a line of demarcation between the
sacred and profane dimensions of life, or between matsuri
(religious rituals) and matsuri-goto (political administration),
both of which were ultimately under the authority of the emperor
who himself was directed by the divine will.[10]

When Buddhism was introduced to Japan in the sixth century
C.E., it was already nearly a thousand years old. Buddhism
equipped Shintō--a primitive religion--with a worthy doctrinal
and ethical content.[11] With its precepts and rules for ethical
and moral behavior, it influenced the thought of the Japanese by
confronting the human misfortunes of sin, sickness, and death
with a new vocabulary that took into account one's circumstance

---

[9] D.C. Holtom, Modern Japan and Shinto Nationalism Revised
ed. (Chicago: University of Chicago Press, 1947) pp. 55,56.

[10] Joseph M. Kitagawa, Religion in Japanese History (New
York: Columbia University Press, 1966) p. 19.

[11] Holtom, p. 129.

7

as being the consequence of one's moral or immoral acts.

According to de Bary:

> With a keener sense of moral responsibility and self-restraint went a growing sense of moral power. New energies were summoned up by the call to a life of discipline, self-mastery, and high aspiration. The life of the spirit, aiming at liberation from the world, replaced the life of the spirits and man's helpless dependence on nature as the basis of religious thought and practice.[12]

Perhaps the assimilation of Buddhist thought with native Shintō teaching took place due to the Buddhist theory of _honji suijaku_ ("true nature manifestation"), and not by some sudden awakening to having been immoral. The _honji suijaku_ theory maintained that Shintō deities were manifestations of Indian Buddhist divinities. Buddhism claimed that the worship of a kami amounted to the worship of a Buddha in its kami form. As Grapard emphasizes:

> The crucial point is that these systematic associations were always established at the level of particular shrines and temples and not at an abstract, national level. In other words, Shintō-Buddhist syncretism remained grounded in each particular religious community, thereby retaining original Shintō characteristics.[13]

One example of Buddhist-Shintō synthesis was the Tendai Shintō (Sannō-Ichijitsu-Shintō) that was located at Enryakuji on Mt. Hiei near Kyoto. In Tendai's philosophy of ultimate reality, primordial Buddha nature as represented by Sākyamuni Buddha was

---

[12] William Theodore de Bary, ed. _The Buddhist Tradition in India, China, and Japan_ (New York: Vintage Books, 1969) pp. 257,258.

[13] Grapard, p. 127.

held to be the reality behind all phenomena, including the kami.
The main deity of the Hiei shrine, the tutelary deity of
Enryakuji was considered an incarnation of Sākyamuni.[14] It was
in this atmosphere of integrative thought that the founders of
later Buddhist sects studied. Priests such as Hōnen, founder of
the Jōdo sect, Shinran of the Jōdo-shin sect, Eisai of the Rinzai
Zen sect, Dōgen of the Soto sect, and Nichiren of the Nichiren
sect, became known as "the five reformers" of Kamakura Buddhism.

Buddhism: Kamakura's Five Reformers

The dominant Buddhist sect at the time was the Tendai that
operated out of the prestigious monastic institution on Mount
Hiei.[15] This temple complex was strongly supported by the
government, and the power and influence it exerted over the
common classes were vast. This led to many internal struggles to
gain control of the most influential "spiritual positions" in the
monastery. These positions of influence were important for
maintaining the economic patronage necessary to operate the
temple. With the political and natural calamities that plagued
the nation, the patronage that was important to the monastery was
consistently threatened to be severed. This was due to the

---

[14] Hirai, p. 280.

[15] This Pure Land teaching propagated the use of nembutsu
(chanting the Buddha's name) in order to receive salvation. The
Buddha referred to here is not Shakyamuni but Amida. Amida was a
bodhisattva who wished to help all sentient beings achieve
Buddhahood. He made forty-eight vows regarding a Buddha land
that he would establish for the faithful following his enlightenment.

9

perception that the rituals performed for the nation were ineffective.

The governmental figures were concerned with maintaining a level of national control. Their pleas to the religious institutions were met with empty rituals. The common classes likewise looked to religion for answers and they naturally turned to their agrarian Shintō folk practices with which they felt they could somehow influence the deities and improve their immediate condition.

The ·Buddhist leaders of the early Kamakura period were aware of what the people needed: salvation from both the social and natural disasters that tormented the nation. The prominent Buddhist figures of the time propagated numerous different teachings regarding individual and national salvation, yet they all had a peculiar commonality: efficacious results based on simple practices. According to Anesaki:

> The Buddhist religion of the new age was not one of ceremonies and mysteries but a religion of simple piety or of spiritual exercise. Dogma gave way to personal experience, ritual and sacerdotalism to piety and intuition, and this new type of religion exerted its influence beyond class limits, exhibiting many democratic features.[16]

The immediate results promised by the new Buddhism, made the religion itself a doctrine that was concerned with the present state of mankind, not just his afterlife. The calamities in Japan during the Buddhist age of mappō could be viewed as a compounded "blessing in disguise" that gave Buddhism an

---

[16] Masaharu Anesaki, _History of Japanese Religion_, p. 168.

opportunity to be propagated further not just as a religion of this world, but more specifically as a religion of the Japanese nation.[17] The five reformers of Kamakura Buddhism differed in their nationalistic perspective in terms of: 1) possible Shintō influence, 2) their perception of Japan (as a divine nation), and 3) specific religious/nationalistic teachings.

Hōnen (1133-1212)

Born the son of a samurai, Hōnen became the first individual to launch the Buddhist reformation of the Kamakura period. He studied at the Enryakuji temple on Mt. Hiei and became a monk of the Tendai sect at age fifteen. Hōnen stressed the aspect of faith over meditation in order for one to receive the benefits of salvation, re-birth into the Pure Land. Hōnen focused on individual salvation and making that path towards salvation accessible to people of all classes.

The nembutsu practice was not exclusive to Hōnen since Heian nobles were known to chant the nembutsu("Namu Amida Butsu") during evening services. Hōnen made the practice an exclusive element in his teachings. His lack of syncretism with indigenous practice was formally condemned in 1205 by the retired Emperor Go-Toba. Wishing to halt the new growing sect of nembutsu exclusivists, the monks at Kofukuji temple presented a document to Go-Toba, known as the Kōfukuji sōjō, that outlined nine points of alleged sacrileges and crimes committed by nembutsu

---

[17] Kitagawa, p. 110.

11

followers.[18] One of these sacrileges was the "error of rejecting the Shintō gods." Hōnen refused to venerate the more famous of historical shrines, thereby breaking an accepted Buddhist link with Japan's indigenous Shintō spiritual past. The last point listed was of a national concern for the retired emperor: the "error of bringing confusion to the nation since the nembutsu practice is not based upon the harmony of the Dharma of the Emperor and Buddha." According to Matsunaga:

> This criticism blames the decline of the eight sects of established Buddhism, with the resulting failure of the Ritsuryo government, solely upon the upsurge of the senju nembutsu movement. What the author actually meant was that a religion arising from the masses naturally upsets the existing authoritarian control, and he used the existing state of political and social confusion as proof of his contention.[19]

Hōnen's break with acknowledging Shintō deities is indicative of his fervent desire to propagate just Buddhism, with an exclusive practice. He focused on Amida's Pure Land as a place to which an individual should desire to go posthumously. His teaching was not "Japan-centered" in the present tense but retained the Buddhist other-world character. Though Hōnen taught that one may receive grace from Amida Buddha and have a re-birth in the Pure Land posthumously, he stressed his "better after-life" teaching in order to provide spiritual solace in the present life and hope for a better one in the next. The solace that Hōnen brought was the idea that through the easy path of

---

[18] Matsunaga, Vol. 2, p. 64.

[19] Ibid, p. 66.

faith all people have an equal opportunity at spiritual
salvation. Hōnen did not propagate a nationalistic teaching in
his nembutsu practice.

Eisai (1141-1215)

Born into a priestly family at the Kibitsu shrine in Bizen,
present day Okayama Prefecture, Myoan Eisai became a monk at
Enryakuji at the age of fourteen. Accepting the Buddhist
teaching of mappō as the explanation for the physical and
spiritual degradation of the nation, Eisai was convinced that
there was an urgent need to revitalize Buddhism in Japan. The
way that this was going to be done was by going to China to re-
discover the true source and teachings of Buddhism. Focusing his
study on T'ien-t'ai (Jp. Tendai) Buddhism, the twenty-eight year
old monk spent only six months in China but returned to Japan
with approximately sixty scrolls of T'ien'-t'ai Buddhist
teachings. In 1187 Eisai went back to China, this time with the
intent of journeying on to India to visit the sacred area
associated with the historical Buddha-Sākyamuni. Unable to
obtain the necessary travel documents from the Chinese
government, Eisai opted to stay on Mt. T'ien-tai for four years
and study under the Ch'an (Jp. Zen) master Hsu-an Huai-ch'ang.

Since meditation (Ind. dhyāna, "mind concentration") is a
practice that was associated with Buddhism from its creation, the
training that Eisai undertook was not new and unfamiliar. The
exclusive practice of his Lin-chi (Jp. Rinzai) school was

13

contemplation of a sound, a word, or a phrase while in seated
meditation (Ch'an hua-t'ou). Though Eisai studied in China he
did not develop a disdain for his own country as being   .
spiritually inferior. He sought a return to a former glorious
age of one's spiritual traditions. According to Kitagawa:

> His chief concern was not with a "certainty of
> salvation" as in the cases of Hōnen, Shinran, and
> Nichiren. His main preoccupation was with the
> purification and restoration of the traditional glories
> of Buddhism in Japan.[20]   .

The "traditional glories of Buddhism in Japan" that Eisai
sought were articulated in his nationalistic teachings that
stressed Buddhism as providing salvation for the state. These
teachings were documented in a text he wrote to defend his
position against Enryakuji accusations that he was attempting to
establish a new heretical sect of Buddhism in Japan. In 1194
Eisai wrote Kōzen gokoku-ron ("Arguments in Favor of the
Promulgation of Zen as a Defense of the Country"). Eisai's
Shintō nationalism is evident in his veneration of the Emperor:

> In our country the Divine Sovereign shines in splendor
> and the influence of his virtuous wisdom spreads far
> and wide. Emissaries from the distant lands of south
> and central Asia pay their respects to his court.[21]

He was loyal to the imperial family in an age of feudal
dissension and declared, "How true it is that our land of Japan
is above all nations, excelling India and China and superior to

---

[20] Kitagawa, pp. 123-124.

[21] de Bary, p. 364.

14

all other countries."[22] Martin Collcutt outlines the Kōzen
gokoku-ron:

> In this long work Eisai offered four major arguments in
> favor of his Zen: that it was the very essence of
> Buddhism; that it was not a new teaching but had been
> accepted by Saicho and other patriarchs of Tendai
> Buddhism; that is was based on the disciplined
> observance of the Buddhist precepts; and that its
> sponsorship would certainly lead to the rejuvenation of
> Buddhism in Japan and to the prosperity and security of
> the nation.[23]

Unlike Hōnen's accessible path of salvation through faith
for all classes, Eisai did not direct his attention toward the
common classes. He sought alliance with the new military
political order which found his strict yet simple teachings
compatible with the new dominant bushi (warrior) class. Hōnen
refused to venerate certain Shintō shrines, yet Eisai praised the
divinity of the Emperor. The reality of economic patronage was
important to Eisai. As the bushi class supported him he was able
to spread his teachings. Since Eisai influenced the neccessary
classes and individuals who would support his propagations, his
teachings could be extended throughout the nation.

Shinran (1173-1263)

The founder of the Jōdo Shin-shu ("True Pure Land Sect") was
born into the family of a minor bureaucrat in the vicinity of
Kyoto. Though specific details about his life are scarce, five

---

[22] Holtom, p. 139.

[23] Martin Collcutt, "Eisai", Encyclopedia of Religion.
Mircea Eliade, ed., (New York: Macmillan Publishing Co.,1987), p.
453.

major periods of his career are recognized. The first is entering the Tendai monastic institution of Enryakuji on Mt. Hiei at the age of eight. For the next twenty years Shinran served as a doso ("menial monk") in the Jōgyō Zammai-dō.[24] The second period was at the age of twenty-nine when he left Mt. Hiei and became a disciple of Hōnen. This term of study led to the third period of Shinran's life-his exile by the government in 1207. Four years later marked the end of his exile by a governmental pardon and Shinran went to Inada in Hitachi Province (present day Ibaraki Prefecture). In 1253 the fifth period of Shinran's life began when he returned to Kyoto and remained there until his death.

It was during his four year exile that Shinran did something that was canonically illegal for a Buddhist cleric to do--marry. This marriage led to Shinran's fathering seven or eight children and accounted for the practice of open, public marriages of clerics to become a common occurrence thereafter. Like his master Hōnen, Shinran had a disdain for the exclusive veneration of Shintō deities. Since the theory of honji-suijaku ("true nature manifestation") was well entrenched in Kamakura religious thought, Shinran's understanding of the indigenous practices were inclusive. According to Matsunaga:

---

[24] This was a chapel of the monastery grounds where the Tendai practice of jogyo-zammai took place. Jogyo-zammai was a method of samadhi or contemplative meditation that involved constant nembutsu while circumambulating a statue of Amida Buddha.

> If we view Shinran's attitude toward the native gods, we note that he first placed them at their proper perspective at the conventional level, admonishing against the type of reliance that leads man to forfeit control over his own destiny. And secondly, at what might be described as the level of Enlightenment or the attainment of _tariki_ ("other power") faith, his attitude was not exclusive, insofar as it did not entail intolerance or rejection. Rather, the gods and all the other Buddhas and Bodhisattvas were embraced _within_ the _nembutsu_, and this attitude was developed by his successors.[25]

Shinran's tolerance of the Kami was possible through his perspective of the position all deities had in relation to man's ability to determine his future. It was in man's capacity to freely choose to have faith in "the gods and all other Buddhas and Bodhisattvas" that Shinran focused on. Once man (and woman) recognized this ability of having faith and freely chose to believe in Amida Buddha, they may be saved because of what _they chose_ to do, not because of what the deity wanted done. It was through faith in Amida Buddha that one can be granted re-birth into the Pure Land. This belief was forged during his exilic period that convinced him that faith is applicable to all classes of people.[26]

Hōnen's teaching of the _nembutsu_ as being an action one must faithfully perform in order to receive Amida's grace was the standard Pure Land teaching. While traditional Buddhist schools understood faith as an inward spiritual movement through which

---

[25] Matsunaga, vol. 2, p. 111.

[26] Honen's teaching was that "even a bad man will be saved how much more a good man!" Shinran took the teaching and reversing it taught, "If even good people can be reborn in the Pure Land, how much more the wicked man." de Bary, p. 332.

17

people aspired to enlightenment, Shinran stressed that the root source of that faith was Amida's compassion manifested sincerely and truly in the mind of the person.[27]

Shinran's teaching of faith in Amida makes evident his focus on the Pure Land and not the "world" (Japan). This hope for salvation is what could have brought a tranquility to the individual and thereby this peaceful state of existence could be manifested in proper relationships resulting in the ultimate peaceful functioning of society. Hōnen sought to influence all classes with nembutsu practice while Eisai felt the "responsible" leaders and aristocrats should be preached to. Shinran's marriage coupled with his teaching of faith in Amida founded a "genuine lay Buddhism by identifying the family system with approved social practice."[28] Shinran's teachings, though they are able to cut across all classes, remain individual in nature. Faith was the full mental realization of Amida's compassion inherent in the individual, not the collective consciousness of the nation. So only if all citizens realized this compassion and this faith, could the nation have been affected, altered, and possibly saved while in the degenerate age of mappō. Like his teacher Hōnen, Shinran did not include a nationalistic teaching in his nembutsu practice.

---

[27] Alfred Bloom, "Shinran", Kodansha Encyclopedia of Japan. (Tokyo: Kodansha International Ltd., 1983), vol. 7, p. 123.

[28] Holtom, p. 139.

18

Dōgen (1299-1253)

Being born into a family of aristocratic status,[29] Dōgen was afforded the opportunity of an excellent education. The traumatic events in his early childhood of the loss of his father (at age two) and his mother (at age seven), greatly affected his outlook on life. He later became a novice Tendai monk at Mt. Hiei and struggled with the concepts of acquired versus inherent enlightenment. He questioned the use of ascetic practices (to acquire enlightenment) since all sentient (thinking, feeling) beings were supposedly endowed with a Buddha nature. The Tendai teachings failed to provide for Dōgen any substantial answer(s) to his questions and so he decided to leave Mt. Hiei in search of the truth. Visiting other monasteries and still being spiritually unsatisfied, he decided on travelling to China to seek a master who could thoroughly answer his questions.

After travelling to a variety of Ch'an (Jp. Zen) monasteries on Mt. T'ien-t'ung, he felt his efforts in finding an answer seemed fruitless. It was during the preparations for the return trip to Japan that Dōgen encountered the cook from the Ts'ao-t'ung (Jp. Soto) monastery who sparked a new sense of urgency in his quest for spiritual answers. The cook informed Dōgen that the new abbot at his monastery was Ju-ching. After arriving at the monastery in 1225, Dōgen saw that the primary spiritual activity emphasized was shikantaza ("just sitting"). This was

---

[29] It is assumed that his father was Koga (or Minamoto) Michichika (d. 1202). Heinrich Dumoulin, Zen Buddhism: A History, Japan. (New York:MacMillan, 1990) p. 51.

based on the account of Shakyamuni's seated meditation under a
"bo" tree that led to his enlightenment. What led to Dōgen's
enlightenment occurred during an evening session of shikantaza
when a monk fell asleep and was abruptly set straight by Ju-ching
when he said, "In Zen, body and mind are cast off. Why do you
sleep?" Upon hearing the phrase shinjin datsuraku ("body and
mind are cast off") Dōgen became enlightened.[30]

Following Ju-ching's validation of his enlightenment, Dōgen
returned to the Kennin-ji temple in Kyoto to promote his imported
Soto Zen teachings. What made Dōgen's Buddhist teachings
different from other existing sects was his conviction that even
in the period of the latter days one may become enlightened, but
by one's own effort (Jp. jiriki), not through the other power
(Jp. tariki) of Amida as taught by the Pure Land sects. Dōgen
was exclusivistic in his early teachings about how one may be
enlightened or not.[31] He made this point perfectly clear in a
portion of his work entitled Bendowa:

---

[30] James Kodera maintains that Dogen may have misunderstood
Ju-ching's statement. This poses problems for the validity of
Dogen's enlightenment experience. As Kodera points out: It must
be noted, however, that Dogen's "dropping the body and mind"
(shinjin datsuraku) does not appear in Ju-ching's collected
sayings. It is known that Ju-ching used the expression "dropping
the dust from the mind," which is pronounced the same way in
Japanese (shinjin datsuraku) but differently from the Chinese:
shen-hsin t'o-lo for "dropping the body and mind" but hsin ch'en
t'o-lo for "dropping the dust from the mind. Takushi James
Kodera, Dogen's Formative Years in China, (Boulder: Prajna Press,
1985), p. 106.

[31] The "how" of his methodology is exclusivistic as well as
the "who" in his post-Echizen writings where he adamantly insists
that only male monastics are capable of becoming enlightened.

20

> Commitment to Zen is casting off body and mind. You
> have no need for incense offerings, homage praying,
> nembutsu, penance disciplines, or silent sūtra
> readings; just sit single mindedly.[32]

The singleminded sitting of zazen was taught as "the right
entrance to the Dharma."[33] This emphasis on zazen was not
accepted enthusiastically by the established sects, which favored
a syncretic approach to Zen practice.[34] Dōgen's severe
reductionism of Buddhist methodology into an isolated practice is
what placed him in the category of a reformer of traditional
Buddhist practices.

Since the Tendai monastery of Enryakuji on Mt. Hiei had a
Buddhist-Shintō syncretic ideology, one may posit that this was
the only place that Dōgen may have had any formal contact with
Shintō teaching and/or veneration. Even though this may have
been the case, the level of influence that any Shintō teaching
may have had on Dōgen can at best be minimal since Dōgen left Mt.
Hiei with more questions to his problems than answers.

It was in China that Dōgen had his enlightenment experience
and not in Japan, so his spiritual loyalty is focused on the
tradition of the religious practice and not on any specific

---

[32] Norman Wadell and Masao Abe, trans. "Dogen's Bendowa" in
The Eastern Buddhist 4 (1971), p. 133. (Also in Martin Collcutt's
Five Mountains.)

[33] Martin Collcut, Five Mountains, The Rinzai Zen Monastic
Institution in Medieval Japan. (Cambridge: Harvard University
Press, 1981), p. 50.

[34] This involved daily zazen sessions followed by traditional Shingon esoteric observances that were devoted to Fudo
Myoo, Aizen Myoo, and the Thousand-Armed Kannon (Collcutt, p.
48).

geographical location. One could also argue the point of Dōgen
being a Sinophile since he became enlightened in China and not
his native Japan. However, it is Dōgen's life and works that
provide a better insight into how he perceives his teaching in
terms of nationalistic implications: stress the importance of the
teaching for the benifit of the nation, but only if the
government provides financial support for propagation of the
teachings.

When Dōgen went to Echizen province in 1243 the dominant
Buddhist establishment attacked the ideologies of the new and
growing movements. As Collcutt points out:

> In an attempt to justify his teaching and defend his
> teaching, Dōgen like Eisai before him, presented to
> Emperor Go-Saga (1220-1272) a tract entitled <u>Gokoku</u>
> <u>Shōbōgi</u> [sic] (Principles of the true Buddhist law in
> defense of the country), in which he argued that, far
> from being a threat, his teachings were positively
> beneficial for the nation.[35]

Dōgen's nationalistic claims may have been made specifically for
the sake of gaining governmental support and patronage. Even if
Zen is an intuitive method of spiritual training with the aim of
attaining a lofty transcendence over worldly care,[36]Dōgen knew
what the importance of gaining financial assistance and
governmental support would have meant for his teaching on a
national level. Yokoi explains:

> Dōgen believed that ideally the state should be based
> on the spirit of Zen Buddhism. The fact that he
> presented the cloistered emperor Gosaga, with the

---

[35] Collcutt, <u>Five Mountains</u>, p. 51.

[36] Anesaki, (<u>History of Japanese Religion</u>), p. 208.

22

treatise <u>Gokoku Shōbō-gi</u> shows how eagerly he tried to teach the national authorities the universality of Zen. His viewpoint of the state was that the citizens thereof should be governed by the spirit of Zen, that is the equality and identity of all things and all people.[37]

Dōgen's message of his Buddhist teachings benefitting the nation were seen as threatening to the established sects. How could Dōgen's Buddhist practice be better for the nation than what the established teaching offered? Commenting on the reason behind Dōgen's being denied governmental support, Collcutt states:

His teaching on the unique efficacy of <u>zazen</u> was described as a dangerously personal interpretation of Buddhism. Continued teaching, it was claimed, would not only undermine the basic foundations of Mahayana Buddhism in Japan but threaten the security of the state.[38]

It was following this rejection by the government that Dōgen became exclusivistic in his teachings by claiming that only monastics may be saved or enlightened. Dōgen also broke ties with possible patrons by making "every effort to avoid contact with men of high rank"[39] and this is where he differs from Eisai and his political adeptness.

Even though Dōgen studied for a time under Eisai, their characters were completely different. Eisai, through his appeal to the aristocracy, did much to make Zen practice acceptable in Japan. He was in this way a personification of the virtue of

---

[37] Yuho Yokoi, <u>Zen Master Dogen</u> (New York: Weatherhill, 1976), p. 40.

[38] Collcutt, p. 52.

[39] Anesaki, (<u>History of Japanese Religion</u>), p. 308.

adaptability, but Dōgen equally personified the opposite virtue in Zen: rugged determination and uncompromising independence.[40] The irony in Dōgen's teaching is that he initially preached equality yet later avoided the aristocracy and critically condemned others for accepting the mappō teaching. As Kitagawa explains:

> Thus, unlike Hōnen, Shinran, and Nichiren, whose teachings were derived from the notion of mappō, Dōgen was persuaded that a true believer has access to the "Perfect Law" of Buddha.[41]

Dōgen felt that depraved and evil people existed in all periods of history, not just in the age of mappō. Dōgen propagated his Zen teachings as being good for the nation but only as he sought patronage. When he was denied support he abandoned his nationalistic teachings and emphasized cloistered monastic practice as the exclusive means of personal salvation.

Conclusion

Each Buddhist reformer had a teaching that promised results if the spiritual practices taught were performed thoroughly and correctly, whether it meant sitting singlemindedly, having absolute faith in Amida Buddha, or chanting the Buddha's name. The teachings were seen as a means to transform the spiritual nature of the believer as well as (for those who taught it)

---

[40] de Bary, p. 357.

[41] Kitagawa, pp. 128-129.

provide divine Buddhist protection for the nation. Most of the reformers who sought patronage received support from at least some wealthy individual. Both Hōnen and Shinran did not fuse their teachings with any nationalism. Dōgen and Eisai propagated nationalism but only Eisai prospered with any substantial patronage and governmental support. As each reformer added his own perspective on Buddhist teaching, a diversity in practice, thought, and doctrine arose. Each reformer was convinced that his way was the true way and that there could be no compromise with his teaching(s). The reformer most noted for his staunch and adamant approach in spreading his teaching is considered as the fifth reformer of Kamakura Buddhism: Nichiren.

CHAPTER II

NICHIREN

The life of a charismatic person who leads a religious movement is often filled with colorful episodes that can either strengthen a preached doctrine or weaken and dismantle the perceived truths. The unique circumstances of Nichiren's life strengthened his sense of purpose. He interpreted these circumstances as divine validations of his spiritual teachings. These circumstances were usually in the form of physical persecutions and official condemnations of his teachings by the established Buddhist sects of the time. Most notable of these persecutions was the incident at Tatsu-no-kuchi on September 12, 1271 where the government attempted to execute him. According to Kitagawa:

> Nichiren's life was full of miraculous events. In 1271 he was tried for high treason. On his way to Tatsu-no-kuchi, he called to Hachiman, the patron kami of the Minamoto clan, to rescue him. According to his own (Nichiren's) account, as he sat on a straw mat, bright lights from heaven blinded the soldiers, so that they became panic stricken and ran away. This convinced Nichiren all the more of his divine mission.[42]

What makes this episode in Nichiren's life so interesting is that even though he is known as a Buddhist reformer, one of the most significant circumstances in his life is attributed to the divine intervention of Hachiman (a Shintō war deity) on his behalf. If a Shintō kami saved Nichiren's life, did that mean the kami • protected the Buddhist reformer because it (Hachiman) serves

---

[42] Kitagawa, ff. 76, p. 119.

Buddhism or did Nichiren call upon Hachiman because he is more powerful than Buddhist deities? The ease with which Nichiren feels he can call upon a patron Shintō kami of a feudalistic clan for personal protection clearly exemplifies the honji suijaku ("true nature manifestation") theory of Buddhist deity-Shintō kami amalgamation. Therefore, Nichiren's life and teachings could be viewed from the perspective of a fusion of Shintō nationalism and Buddhist salvific rhetoric.

But what caused the castigation of Nichiren? Were his teachings so heretical or powerfully truthful that Nichiren challenged the world views of the established Buddhist sects? In order to gain a better understanding of why Nichiren preached his form of Buddhism as a means of national security, an examination of his life through a Buddhist and Shintō perspective will provide some insight to his unique world view and how his world view led him to propagate his bold teachings.

Nichiren's Life: A Buddhist-Shintō Fusion.

On February 16, 1222 Nichiren "was born poor and lowly to a chandala family"[43] in a small fishing village called Kominato, which was located in Awa province (present day Chiba prefecture in Southeast Japan). According to Rodd:

---

[43] Chandala (Caṇḍala) is the lowest class in the Indian caste system. This class was actually lower than the caste system, and it was comprised of people who were required to kill living creatures as part of their profession. The Gosho Translation Committee, ed., trans., The Major Writings of Nichiren Daishonin, Vol. 1 (Tokyo: Nichiren Shoshu International Center, 1982), p. 37.

Nichiren's lowly origins were unique among the religious leaders of the Middle Ages in Japan; Hōnen, Shinran, Dōgen, and Eisai all came from noble or samurai families. Moreover, Nichiren was born far from the centers of political or religious influence while the others were all from Kyoto or the surrounding provinces. Such a birth was a handicap in a society in which the religious hierarchy was based upon social status, and the great centers of Buddhism lay in the Western provinces of Japan.[44]

So even from his birth Nichiren was contradicting the established patterns of social and spiritual approval and validation. Nichiren's birthplace was important in relation to his future teachings because it (Kominato) was an estate of the Ise Shrine (Ise Jingu) where the ancestral gods of the Imperial family are enshrined.[45] The sacred atmosphere undoubtably served to stimulate his awareness of Japanese tradition and strong feelings of nationalism.[46] On the sixteenth day of the second month in 1275 Nichiren wrote the following while in exile:

---

[44] Laurel Rasplica Rodd, Nichiren: Selected Writings (Honolulu: University of Hawaii Press, 1980), p. 4.

[45] Ise's inner shrine is said to date from the third century, C.E. and to contain Amaterasu-Omi-Kami, the mythical ancestor of the Imperial family. Amaterasu is represented by the sacred mirror (yata no kagami), one of the three Imperial regalia.

[46] Alicia and Daigan Matsunaga, Foundation of Japanese Buddhism, Vol. 2 (Los Angeles and Tokyo: Buddhist Books International, 1976), p. 137.

The area of Tojo in the province of Awa is a remote
place but it appears to be the centre of Japan. The
reason is because Amaterasu O Mikami [sic] dropped her
manifestation (suijaku) there. Originally in the past
she dropped her manifestation at Ise but the rulers of
the nation offered her little respect while profoundly
venerating Hachiman and the Kamo gods, therefore she
was angered. Minamoto Yoritomo by petition ordered
Kodayu of Auga to receive her and the outer shrine at
Ise was reverently and secretly brought to this place
satisfying Amaterasu, and thus he became Shogun holding
all of Japan in his hands. This man set the area of
Tojo as the residence of Amaterasu O Mikami and
therefore the great god does not reside in Ise but
rather in the Tojo area of Awa province... Nichiren, in
the Tojo area, province of Awa in Japan of Jambudvipa,
for the first time has begun to propagate the true
Dharma.[47]

Nichiren worshipped the Sun Goddess Amaterasu[48] and he

considered many Japanese kami the spirits of past emperors.[49]

For Nichiren the divine lineage of the Emperor meant divine

protection for the nation but only if the rulers' claim to

authority is a legitimate one. Japanese historian Masaharu

Anesaki commented on Nichiren:

He declared that the nation would be ruined, unless the
fundamental principle of the national life should be
restored, that is, unless the people were governed by
rulers legitimate both in title and authority.[50]

The legitimacy in title and authority could only be brought

about in one way - by understanding and knowing the proper

---

[47] Ibid., p. 137.

[48] Charles A. Moore, ed., Philosophy and Culture: East and
West (Honolulu: University of Hawaii Press, 1968), p. 104.

[49] Koichi Shinohara, "Religion and Political Order in
Nichiren's Buddhism," Japanese Journal of Religious Studies 8
(1981): p. 232.

[50] Masaharu Anesaki, Nichiren: The Buddhist Prophet (Gloucester, MA: Peter Smith, 1966), p. 7.

29

lineage of the Emperor and his heirs. Nichiren felt a need to question the legitimacy of the Emperor's lineage because he was concerned about the problems of peace in the country, particularly in relation to the death of the boy-Emperor Antoku, whose divine personage should have assured him divine protection and assistance from the gods.[51] Like all Kamakura leaders Nichiren was forced to address the issue of the native deities (kami) and the divine political plan for the nation. Since Nichiren's early life was in an area significant to Shintō practice, it was natural for Nichiren to accept the notion of Japan being a divine country inhabited by deities. The kami were native to Japan, and in order for Nichiren to influence the common people, he had to explain a relationship between native kami and Buddhist deities. The technique he incorporated was based on a widely used theory of honji-suijaku ("true nature manifestation"). He considered every Shintō god commencing from the Sun Goddess to be a suijaku ("manifestation") of the Eternal Sākyamuni of the Lotus Sūtra, and he also believed that the gods had an obligation to punish their enemies.[52] The parallel between the status of the Buddha and the status of the kami was made more explicit in a passage where Nichiren stated that the god Hachiman, the spirit of Ojin, the sixteenth emperor, was the

---

[51] Baird and Bloom, p. 274.

[52] Matsunaga, pp. 167-168.

30

"trace" or incarnation of the "original substance" of Sākyamuni Buddha.[53]

The calamities that plagued Japan became the impetus that moved Nichiren to propagate forcefully the pan-sectarian Buddhist teaching of sokushin jōbutsu ("the attainment of Buddhahood in the present body and lifetime").[54] This teaching gave an immediate solution which would appeal to both the common people and the ruling class in light of the many calamities and heresies throughout the country. But Nichiren believed that the native gods abandoned Japan because of the numerous heresies that were propagated and because of the invalid spiritual lineage of the ruling class. These heresies accounted for the political and natural disasters in the nation. At this point, Buddhism provided a spiritual and chronological explanation for Japan's multitudinous problems.

Nichiren justified his position by pointing to the corrupt intrigues of sects in opposition to him in light of a Buddhist doctrinal reality of his time, mappō. This "Age of the Latter Law" was considered to be a period of decadent religious and

---

[53] Shinohara, p. 232.

[54] Was there any conflict between Shinto folk beliefs and Buddhist beliefs during the Kamakura period? In a lecture on "The Special Characteristics of Japanese Religion," Shigekiyo Okada pointed out that during the Kamakura period there was no conflict between veneration of Shinto kami and veneration of Buddhist deities. This syncretism of powerful deities is the teaching of sanjuban shinsetsu ("thirty deities who take turn in protecting the Lotus Sutra"). Shigekiyo Okada, "The Special Characteristics of Japanese Religion." East-West Center, Honolulu, 20 Sept. 1991.

governmental activities. These activities caused Nichiren to attempt to influence state policy through his religious views.[55]

But how was Nichiren able to attack the opposing sects and then question the legitimacy of the Emperor's lineage? First, he needed to claim some kind of spiritual authority in order to provide a foundation for his attack on existing worldly matters. Nichiren was able to do this by using two methods to validate his fundamentalist teachings. The first method was to clarify his own teachings with the "T'ien-t'ai Kyōhan" or the comparative classification of the sūtras.[56] Nichiren uses passages from the following sūtras in order to validate his teachings of healing the nation's ills with his form of Buddhist practice: Konkomyo, Daijuku, Ninno, Yakushi, Nirvāna, Kegon, and Lotus, (Saddharma pundarîka). He used this method not only to validate the truths in his teachings but to point out how previous and existing sects have distorted Buddhist teaching and practice. In his work, the Risshōankokuron ("On Securing the Peace of the Land Through the Propagation of True Buddhism") one of Nichiren's characters points out the effectiveness of the T'ien-t'ai Kyōhan methodology by saying:

> Now by citing passages from a wide variety of
> scriptures, you have clearly demonstrated the rights
> and wrongs of the matter. Therefore I have completely

---

[55] Ibid, p. 275.

[56] Jackie Stone, "Seeking Enlightenment in the Last Age: Mappo Thought in Kamakura Buddhism, Part II." The Eastern Buddhist 18 (1985): p. 44.

forsaken my earlier mistaken convictions, and my ears
and eyes have been opened on point after point.[57]

Nichiren supported his claims and statements with passages
from various scriptures of established sects yet later condemned
them as being false practices and heretical. The irony of
Nichiren's systematic approach of searching for "seeds of truth"
in the writings of other sects was in his use of tradition at a
time when he condemned other existing practices. The significance
of his having used this methodology is that he apparently did not
wish to present a neo-Buddhist teaching but rather a true
Buddhist teaching which he felt he alone was destined to reveal
in the age of mappō. By quoting specific passages from
scriptures of established sects, Nichiren was able to draw the
prospective convert to his teachings by transfering his attention
from one Buddhist perspective of alleged partial truth over to
his perspective of complete truth.

The second method was a hermeneutical technique in which he
placed himself within the Lotus Sūtra and insisted that his
interpretations were scripturally valid. Referring to a chapter
in the Lotus Sūtra in which the two Buddhas Prabhūta-ratna and
Tathāgata Sākyamuni hold counsel, Nichiren stated:

> I, Nichiren, was not present there in the congregation,
> and yet there is no reason to doubt the statements of
> the Scripture. Or, is it possible that I was there?
> Common mortal that I am, I am not well aware of the
> past, yet in the present I am unmistakably the one who
> is realizing the Lotus of Truth. Then in the future I
> am surely destined to participate in the communion of

---

[57] The Gosho Translation Committee, The Major Writings of
Nichiren Daishonin v. 2, p. 41.

the Holy Place. Inferring the past from the present and the future, I should think that I must have been present at the communion in the sky. (The present assures the future destiny, and the future destiny is inconceivable without its cause in the past). The present, future, and past cannot be isolated from one another.[58]

The issue of identity for Nichiren was finding his "true" spiritual identity through subjective scriptural interpretation, thus validating his teachings. In fact, Nichiren believed that he was the Jōgyō Bosatsu promised by Sākyamuni Buddha, and Jōgyō would appear in the age of mappō as written in the Lotus Su̅tra.[59] In his work, the Kaimoku-shō ("Open your eyes to the Lotus Sūtra"), Nichiren stated:

For I perfectly fit the Buddha's description of the person spreading the Lotus Sūtra "in the dreadful and evil world" at the beginning of the Latter Age.[60]

Nichiren was concerned with his sense of identity as being based in the Lotus Sūtra. Kitagawa stated:

To him the transmission of the Lotus Sūtra was based on a "spiritual succession from one charismatic person to the next, even though there might be a long time span between them. Thus Nichiren considered himself, on one hand, the successor to the transmission of the "Sākyamuni-Chih-i [founder of the T'ien-t'ai school in China]-Dengyo" line, and, on the other, also the · incarnations of Visiṣṭacāritra Bodhisattva (Jōgyō, in Japanese, to whom Sākyamuni is said to have entrusted the Lotus Sūtra).[61]

---

[58] Anesaki, Nichiren: The Buddhist Prophet, p. 84.

[59] Baird and Bloom, p. 274.

[60] Nichiren Daishonin, Kaimoku-sho, ed. and trans. Kyotsu Hori (Tokyo: Nichiren Shu Overseas Propagation Promotion Association, 1987), p. 108.

[61] Kitagawa, p. 120.

Nichiren felt that Japan should turn to the original Buddha (now manifested in the Lotus Sūtra and consequently the phrase namu-myōhō-renge-kyō) for proper teaching and realize its true identity and sense of nationhood. Nichiren did not stop at making strong parallels with historical texts and scriptural figures. He likened the Lotus Sūtra to a national Japanese Shintō treasure. In his work, the Senji-shō ("Selecting the Right Time"), Nichiren stated:

> Moreover, receiving the imperial edict defining the Lotus Sūtra, the Konkōmyō-Kyō (Sūtra of the Golden Light), and the Ninnō-kyō (Sūtra of the Benevolent King) to be the three sūtras for the tranquility of the nation, the Grand master enshrined them at Shinkan-in (main hall of Enryaku-ji) to be revered forever as though they were the Three Imperial Regalias [sic] (a divine jewel, a treasured sword, and a sacred mirror enshrined in the imperial sanctuary), the most precious of all treasures in Japan.[62]

The subtlety of Nichiren's Shintō nationalistic rhetoric is evident in how he paralleled the Lotus Sūtra with a divine jewel (fitting, since there is a parable of "the jewel" in the Lotus

---

[62] Nichiren Daishonin, Senji-sho, ed. and trans. Kyotsu Hori (Tokyo: Nichiren Shu Overseas Propagation Promotion Association, 1989) 152. The three Imperial Regalias: a sword (Ame-nö-Murökömo-nö-Tsurugi), a mirror (Yasaka-nö-Kagami), and a curved jewel (Yasaka-Ni-nö-Magötöma) were used to lure the Sun (Goddess-Amaterasu) out of a cave whose hiding had created a darkness that threatened the life of the universe.

Sūtra).[63] Later in the _Senji-shō_ he made an interesting

clarification on the divinity of Japan as a whole. He stated:

> Queen Māyā gave birth to Prince Siddhārtha after
> dreaming she was pregnant with the Sun. So the
> Buddha's infant name was Sun-seed. This country is
> called Japan, meaning the origin of the sun because
> Goddess Amaterasu, the founder of Japan, is the Goddess
> of the Sun.[64]

At this point, one begins to see the Shintō nationalism

expressed through the rhetoric of Nichiren's Buddhism. For

someone like Nichiren, who forged his sense of purpose by

subjective scriptural interpretation,[65] thus seeking a spiritual

ancestral lineage to validate his present teachings, Antoku's

death was a harsh reality and a stark contrast to the lofty ideal

of divine lineage protected by the gods. The Emperor of Japan

was dead. What did that mean for the security and future of the

nation? Because of Antoku's death, Nichiren did not propagate

Shintō nationalism but rearticulated its same ethno-spiritual

---

[63] In Roll Four, Chapter Eight ("Receipt of Prophecy by Five
Hundred Disciples") the parable of the jewel contains a verse
that shows how Nichiren used the Lotus Sutra as the vehicle for
salvation. "Now you need only take this jewel, exchange it for
what you need, and have things always as you wish, suffering
neither want nor shortage." Leon Hurvitz, trans. _Scripture of
the Lotus Blossom of the Fine Dharma_ (New York: Columbia University Press, 1976), p. 165.

[64] Daishonin, _Senji-sho_, p. 164.

[65] Daishonin, _Kaimoku-sho_ p. 108. In chapter five Nichiren
also stated, "However, if only I, Nichiren, had not been born in
this country, the twenty line verse of the thirteenth chapter,
'The Encouragement of Keeping this Sutra,' in the fifth fascicle
of the _Lotus Sutra_ would be empty words and the Buddha would
almost be a great liar."

36

emphasis with the vocabulary of his redefined, Buddhist teachings.

Aside from his concern for proper political/divine lineage as it applied to the Emperor, Nichiren questioned the very nature of Buddhism. He was concerned with the pluralism of sects, the tremendous volumes of sūtras, and the contradictory nature of propagated spiritual methodologies. He eventually concluded that "just as a nation cannot function with two rulers, if Buddhism is to be effective there can only be one true sect and one true sūtra."[66] He believed the destiny of the state depended on its adherence to the true form of Buddhism.[67]

How did Nichiren conclude that his teaching would be the most efficacious for the nation? His research began at the age of eleven when he entered a temple on Mt. Kiyozumi, less than ten miles north of his village (Kominato). When Nichiren was sixteen, he left Mt. Kiyozumi for a study tour. In his later writings Nichiren stated:

---

[66] Matsunaga, p. 138.

[67] Baird and Bloom, p. 275.

37

> I traveled to study at the temples of different
> provinces, in Kamakura, Kyoto, at Mount Hiei, Mount
> Kōya, Onjōji, Tennōji, and others.... I had one wish:
> that I might learn all the teachings of the Buddha
> which had been brought to Japan, all the discussions by
> Bodhisattvas and commentaries by teachers. Not only
> were there the Kusha, Jōjitsu, Ritsu, Hōsso, Sanron,
> Kegon, Shingon, and Tendai schools, but also the ones
> called Zen and Jōdo. Since I wanted to learn at least
> the central teachings, even if I did not understand the
> complexities of doctrine of each school, I traveled
> extensively....[68]

It was in Kamakura that Nichiren's compassion and concern
for the nation was heightened. There were plagues, droughts,
famines, typhoons, fires, earthquakes, political plots,
uprisings, and terrifying astronomical events such as an eclipse
and a comet.[69] The religious institutions of the time were
approached by the government to perform rituals and services to
end the calamities that befell the nation, but few services, if
any, were effective. In the medieval context religion was
recognized as a powerful force for both society and the
individual, and it was capable of producing material benefits and
personal liberation.[70] From the time that Buddhism was
introduced to Japan in the sixth century, it was adopted as a
political tool as well as a method of salvation. Various sūtras,
including the Lotus Sūtra, were referred to as "nation-protecting
sūtras." These texts promised the protection of various gods to

---

[68] Rodd, p. 5.

[69] Ibid, p. 8.

[70] James C. Dobbins, "Envisioning Kamakura Buddhism." Prepared for the Annual Meeting of the Society for the Study of
Japanese Religions held at the Marriot Hotel, New Orleans; April
12, 1991; p. 6.

whatever country revered the sūtra.[71] A division between "church
and state" existed as long as the religious leaders failed in
their rituals and services to provide the necessary spiritual
protection for the nation. When the dominant sects provided the
efficacious liturgies for their patrons (the government) and the
desired results were satisfactory, the temple hierarchy was
substantially supported and rewarded. The propagation of
religious truth and specific teachings became a decisive struggle
that took place within the realm of politics.

     In order for Nichiren to propagate his teaching so that it
would become effective on the national scale that he wished, he
had to influence the state and get its support. Nichiren
succeeded to some degree in influencing the state, but the
dominant religious sects did not appreciate his criticizing their
"patron," the government, even if it meant debating their
spiritual ineffectiveness with Nichiren. The religious leaders
were so incensed by Nichiren's condemnations that their
persecutions of him ranged from doctrinal criticism to an attempt
at execution.

     As the Lotus Sūtra was considered a "nation-protecting
sūtra," Nichiren found his validation for adamantly propagating
it. He quotes scripture in allusion to his tormentors as being
part of the process that legitimates and strengthens his sense of
purpose. In his Kaimoku-Shō he stated:

----

[71] Rodd, p. 9.

> The verse says, "Ignorant people will speak ill of us, and threaten us with swords or sticks." Looking at the world today, is there any Buddhist priest other than I, Nichiren, who is spoken ill of, abused, and threatened with swords or sticks on account of the Lotus Sūtra? If, I Nichiren were not here, this verse would be a false prediction.[72]

When Nichiren's enemies succeeded in gaining support from the government for the condemnation of his teachings, Nichiren was quick to substantiate his present torment through scriptural reference. He further wrote:

> As the words of the Sūtra correspond with me, the deeper I fall into disgrace with the shogunate, the greater my pleasure is.[73]

Nichiren's talent lay in his ability not only to justify his teachings by comparative classification of literary texts, but also to take a defeat and turn it into a victory. Regarding his persecution, he stated:

> Affirming divine intervention in favor of a practitioner, the Lotus Sūtra says: "Heavenly servants will come to serve the man who upholds the Lotus Sūtra, swords and sticks will not injure him, and poisons will not harm him"; "His life in this world will be peaceful and he will be reborn in a better place in the future"; or "He will be rewarded with happiness in this present world."[74]

The emphasis that Nichiren has for his focus for salvation is on "this present world." His concern for the situation of Kamakura Japan is evident in the urgent tone of his writings.

---

[72] Nichiren Daishonin, Kaimoku-Sho, p. 108.

[73] Ibid, p. 112.

[74] Ibid, p. 286.

40

CHAPTER III

NATIONALISM IN NICHIREN'S WRITINGS

A prolific writer, Nichiren produced many works in his
lifetime in order to validate and propagate his thought. The
basic theme that permeates his published texts and epistles is
one of nationalism through proper identity. Proper identity is
the full realization that individuals are citizens of a specific
nation (Japan) that has a unique spiritual purpose (to propagate
true Buddhism) which is based on a correct and proper religious
practice (Nichiren's interpretation of the Lotus Sūtra) that has
a profound impact on both the individual (bettering one's life)
and the nation (divine power and protection). Nichiren's primary
concern was not the propagation of Buddhism merely for Buddhism's
sake, but rather for the sake of the people, the nation itself.
This interest with the welfare of the nation stems from the
Shintō teaching of kami inhabiting the land and therefore the
nation and its citizens are to be participants in a mutual
cooperation of proper spiritual efforts in order to produce a
peaceful atmosphere on earth coupled with divine protection from
the heavens.

Nichiren is concerned with the present state of man and the
nation. Nichiren's reasoning for an individual's pursuit of true
Buddhist practice is motivated by the eventual good this pursuit
will have for the whole community, the whole nation. In the
introduction to The Major Writings of Nichiren Daishonin Vol.1,
the editors summarize Nichiren's thought:

41

According to his teaching the workings of the universe are all subject to a single principle or law. By understanding that law, the individual can unlock the hidden potential of his own life and achieve perfect harmony with his environment.[75]

But what exactly is a "perfect harmony" with one's environment? Is it a spiritual harmony or a political harmony that Nichiren sought? Nichiren's teachings stressed a peaceful cooperation between individuals as well as a synergistic relationship between nation and deities. This was possible by tapping into the "single principle or law" which controls the universe and consequently brings the harmonious peace of the cosmos into one's life, society, and nation. The methodology of following Nichiren's teachings to experience peace was to first wholeheartedly accept the teachings, secondly to have absolute faith in the efficaciousness of the practice, and thirdly to practice, which consisted of chanting the daimoku, spreading the teaching through shakubuku, and acknowledging any personal persecution as validation of the Lotus Sūtra teachings. The irony in Nichiren's teaching is that he teaches harmony through coercive means. From Nichiren's perspective, his thoughts, motives and actions were most harmonious with what he interpreted to be good for the nation. Nichiren saw the opposing sects as hindrances to achieving a national harmony. The opposing sects, however, did not agree with his teachings. Rather than attempt to convince peacefully and convert the believers of other sects

---

[75] The Seikyo Times, ed., trans., The Major Writings of Nichiren Daishonin (Vol.1, Tokyo: Nichiren Shoshu International Center,1979), p. xxxii.

he openly condemned them. Nichiren "declared emphatically that believers in the Pure Land teaching would go to hell; that the Zen sect had been created by devils; that Shingon was the ruination of the state; and that the Ritsu sect betrayed the country."[76] Commenting on Nichiren and his time, Anesaki states:

> It was under these circumstances that Nichiren appeared on the public platform as a spokesman of the patriotic cause whose utterances were deeply tinged with religious fervor.[77]

His approach to achieving harmony in the nation can be described as forceful and adamant. Nichiren's uncompromising character is evident in his unbending criticism of other contemporary Buddhist groups, but this trait is even more strongly accentuated in his own movement.[78] Nichiren's movement did not seek to modify or improve existing religious practice but blatantly preached a return to fundamental Buddhist practice as taught in the Lotus Sūtra. More importantly, Nichiren interpreted the Lotus Sūtra teachings to suit his own needs. The troubled atmosphere of the Kamakura period produced a variety of new Buddhist leaders and religious doctrines. Nichiren's urgency is evident not only in his writings but also in how he presents his teachings.

---

[76] Baird and Bloom, p. 270.

[77] Anesaki, Nichiren: The Buddhist Prophet, p. 7.

[78] H. Byron Earhart, Japanese Religion: Unity and Diversity, 3rd ed.(Belmont, California: Wadsworth Publishing Company, 1982), p. 97.

Nichiren's Principle of Spiritual Conversion: Shakubuku

The way that Nichiren propagated his teachings was through shakubuku, "forced conversion or a way of aggressively conquering evil."[79] Nichiren quotes Grand Master T'ien-t'ai from his commentary on the Lotus Sūtra (Fa-hua wen-chu) to validate this method:

> Although the `Peaceful Practices' chapter mainly preaches the gentle means of propagation, another chapter of the Lotus Sūtra says that anyone who does harm to the practitioner of the Lotus would have his head split into seven pieces. Thus, this sūtra also endorses aggressive means.[80]

This passage seems to have a defensive, retaliatory tone rather than an aggressive one. This indicates that Nichiren's actions must have followed the philosophy of "a good offense is a better defense." A historical incident points to this philosophy clearly.

In 1275 the Ikegami brothers became adherents of Nichiren's teaching, and their father, Yasumitsu, disowned the elder son Munenaka for supporting Nichiren's propagations. The younger son, Munenaga, was given the choice of denouncing his faith in Nichiren's teaching in order remain in the family or be disowned. Nichiren wrote a letter to both sons that he addressed as "Letter to the Brothers," telling Munenaka and Munenaga that faith in the

---

[79] Baird and Bloom, p. 275.

[80] Nichiren Daishonin, Kaimoku-Sho, p. 316.

Lotus Sūtra will invariably invite the persecution of others and urging them never to retreat.[81]

This seemed to work with the father for a while as Yasumitsu rescinded his son's banishment. However in 1277 he disowned the son again. This time, Nichiren wrote a letter to Munenaga telling him that he should not discard his faith just to curry favor with his father and win an inheritance, but that he should continue his faith until his father became a believer.[82] Eventually Yasumitsu converted (1278). This historical account points to an example of what the power of shakubuku may be. Adamancy and steadfastness in the faith indicates to the persecutor (or potential convert) the strength that one acquires by adhering to Nichiren's Lotus Sūtra teachings.

Shakubuku was the spiritual and political weapon for Nichiren's teachings and with this approach he was able to "attack" the spiritual and social perspective of the people during the Kamakura period, which was filled with frequent warfare, political scandals, and religious strife. In the epilogue of his Kaimoku-Shō, Nichiren quotes from the Mo-ho chih-kuan:

> There are two opposing ways of spreading Buddhism: the aggressive and persuasive. Such statements in the `Peaceful Practices' chapter as `do not be critical of others' represents the persuasive way, while such words of the Nirvāṇa Sūtra as `arm yourselves with swords and sticks, and behead those who break the teaching of the

---

[81] Yasuji Kirimura, The Life of Nichiren Daishonin (Tokyo: Nichiren Shoshu International Center,1980), pp. 87-88.

[82] Ibid, p. 88.

Buddha' stand for the aggressive way. Though these two
ways are opposite in nature, they both benefit the
people.[83]

Armed with this textual validation for his teaching, proof of

shakubuku's efficaciousness in a time that was fitting for the

propagation of a nationalistic teaching, Nichiren spread his

teaching with the hope that the conversion of a few key figures

in government would signify state acceptance of his doctrine as a

recognized religion, and he would be acknowledged as a

participant in the effort to maintain the spiritual security of

the state.[84] From his writings it is clear that this was his

motive for his propagations. But in an attempt to further

understand Nichiren's nationalism, we should again consider the

Shintō nationalistic ideology in Nichiren's works. This is where

one can see the Shintō tendencies of Nichiren in his redefinition

of the ethno-spiritual nationalism of Shintō with Buddhist

vocabulary.

Nichiren: The Religious Politician

The unification of church and state had always been a

concern of both the governing aristocracy as well as the dominant

Buddhist sects. If the state accepts a particular sect's

teaching and subsidizes its leaders with temples and tax-free

land holdings, is the state serving Buddhism or is Buddhism

serving the state?

---

[83] Nichiren Daishonin, Kaimoku-Sho, p. 312.

[84] Baird and Bloom, p. 275.

46

The various teachings of the Kamakura period reformers, make it evident that they needed the economic patronage of the aristocracy if they were to have any chance of expanding successfully. Hōnen was formally condemned by the retired Emperor Go-Toba. Eisai was politically adept at gaining patronage. Shinran broke from traditional celibacy for monks and married, thereby focusing his teachings on the nuclear family. Shinran was not concerned with nationalism and basically had an apathetic attitude towards it. Dōgen did his best to avoid "men of high rank" following the government's denial of granting him support. Nichiren openly challenged the government, yet sought the conversion of politically influential figures.

What is unfortunate for the Kamakura reformers is that the state seemed to have the final say on whether or not their teachings prospered. The five reformers were not unique in being persecuted by dominant political powers when their teachings were unaccepted. The aristocracy in Japan is historically known for regulating the spiritual life of the nation's inhabitants-even from Buddhism's inception in Japan (552 C.E.) when sūtras and statues of the Buddha were sent from Korea. As Matsunaga points out:

> According to one account, the new faith was proscribed by the Emperor shortly after the Soga accepted it in the belief that the native gods had been offended and caused an outbreak of plague; the Buddha image was subsequently thrown into the Naniwa canal (Nihonshoki: Kimmei, 13th year, 10th month).[85]

---

[85] Matsunaga, Vol. 1, p. 11.

The nation/state therefore has authority over the spiritual teachings propagated, and if the country's leaders validate their lineage through a blood line of previous kami, then Shintō thought ultimately remains in power. Though the five reformers were concerned with truth in their teachings, unless they were supported by the state, their truths remained nationally invalid.

As pointed out earlier, Nichiren's prime concern was with the present decadent condition of Japan and what he could do about it. It was true that Nichiren was a Buddhist monk with a Buddhist agenda, but if the state, a Shintō power, did not acknowledge and patronize Nichiren, what good were his teachings then? The Shintō state had to accept the Buddhist teachings, and this was Nichiren's primary goal: to appease the influential figures who could allow his teachings to serve the nation.

Nichiren's Affirmation of Shintō

Shintō nationalism is evident in his work Risshōankokuron ("On Securing the Peace of the Land Through the Propagation of True Buddhism"), which deals with a concern for the nation. Nichiren's text takes the form of a dialogue between a host (Nichiren's viewpoint) and a travelling guest (Hōjō Tokiyori, a powerful retired regent of his time wielding much influence over matters of religion and state). The host quickly makes his point known concerning the unnatural condition that Japan is in and why this is so:

If we look about, we find the sun and moon continue to move in their accustomed orbits, and the five planets follow their prospective course. Then why is it that the world has already fallen into decline and that the laws of the state have come to an end? What is wrong? What error has been committed?[86]

Nichiren answers this in a later passage that deals with people who no longer follow the true teachings and acknowledge the false doctrines as correct. He states:

In turn, the benevolent deities and sages abandon the nation and leave their accustomed places. As a result, demons and followers of heretical doctrines create disaster and inflict calamity upon the populace.[87]

Nichiren does not specifically state who or what the "benevolent deities" are. The characters for "benevolent deities" (zen shin) in the original text are 善神 .[88] This term has an element of ambiguity in it since it is used by both Buddhists and Shintōists. However, the context within which Nichiren places this term is clearly Shintō if he is referring to deities who "abandon the nation and leave their accustomed places." The "accustomed places" that the deities inhabit are all the natural phenomena associated with Shintō kami: the mountains, trees, wind, certain rock formations, and various waterfalls.

Perhaps it is due to the audience he is addressing (Hōjō Tokiyori) that he does not overtly refer to Shintō kami, but the

---

[86] Major Writings, Vol. 2, p. 5.

[87] Ibid, p. 13.

[88] Kansei Tamura, Nichiren: Risshoankokuron (Tokyo: Tokuma Shoten, 1973), p. 46.

49

argument is supported with Buddhist terminology that seems to be much better suited in battling the heretical teachings responsible for the nation's calamities, as well as for gaining a foothold with a potential patron or individual of influence. This text is concerned with the proper relations of state to religion, in that order. The basic premise of the text is that the adherence to other Buddhist sects has produced calamities for the nation. Reference to Shintō teachings are found in this work because the text emphasizes not salvation or enlightenment but rather national well being (a Shintō concern). Yet the rhetoric remains Buddhist. The focus therefore is that "one should first pray for the welfare of the country"[89] since "the Japanese nation had been founded by the gods (kami) and preserved by an unbroken line of emperors who maintained the unity of religion and state."[90]

From the approach and methodology used by Nichiren, one may conclude that his Shintō nationalism is strongly alluded to yet never overtly stated in distinct Shintō terminology. If we were to compare and contrast his Shintō inferences to his Buddhist propagations, various similarities develop:

---

[89] Shinohara Koichi, "Religion and Political Order in Nichiren's Buddhism" in <u>Japanese Journal of Religious Studies</u> (Vol. 8, 1981, Nagoya: Nanzan Institute for Religion and Culture), p. 229.

[90] Earhart, p. 152.

SHINTO	BUDDHIST
A) Worshipped Amaterasu.	A) Worshipped historical Buddha.
B) Revered the Emperor.	B) Revered the <u>Lotus Sūtra</u>.
C) Made Buddhist texts analogous with Shintō sacred objects.	C) Identified himself as Jōgyō the boddhisattva in scripture.
D) Despised the Shogunate.	D) Despised other sects.

Nichiren was concerned with authenticity and the truth of whom he should worship. He referred to the historical Buddha as being the source for true Buddhist teaching. Likewise he turns to Amaterasu as being Japan's source of origin. He revered the Emperor due to his divine lineage to Amaterasu, and he revered the <u>Lotus Sūtra</u> as being the divine reincarnated, transformed body of the Buddha, the sūtra that embodied a direct lineage back to the Buddha. He made the <u>Lotus Sūtra</u> analogous to the Shintō national treasures and likewise he himself is now either a national treasure, a personified kami, or both. He despised the authority of the Shogunate and other sects, especially if they disagreed with his thought and openly persecuted him; yet he was able to find solace in scripture that validated his persecutions as being predictable consequences of his propagation of a true practice that can benefit the nation of Japan. By using a Shintō nationalistic perspective in his teachings, Nichiren's propagations were strongly geared towards being accepted by the state as an alternative solution to the allegedly ineffective practices of the established Buddhist sects and accepted Shintō traditions. Nichiren provided a new perspective of what a divine nation like Japan is in relation to a religion such as Buddhism, and he presented his teachings in a manner that he hoped would appeal to the nationalistic consciousness of the Shintō state as well as to the spiritual consciousness of the opposition sects. The former method was through subtle implications while the latter was through the shakubuku method of coercive and forceful means.

Even though Nichiren's propagations spoke of Buddhist salvific possibilities, his teachings were strongly nationalistic. It has been argued, however, that Nichiren was not primarily interested in a nationalistic cause but rather in the Buddha-Dharma. Jackie Stone refers to Nichiren's nationalism as being a product of "scholarly assumptions"[91] and "stereotyped accounts of Nichiren that recur in both Japanese and Western scholarship."[92] Stone feels that the nationalism of Nichiren is a late Meiji through World War II construction that in no way reflects the true spiritual emphasis of Nichiren's teaching. As Stone points out:

> The nationalistic readings of Nichiren that flourished during the modern imperial period do not in fact find much support in Nichiren's own writing's which clearly accord primacy to the Buddha-Dharma over national concerns.[93]

---

[91] Jackie Stone, "Reexamining Stereotypes in the Study of Nichiren: Nationalism, Intolerance, and Independence from Tendai." Prepared for the Annual Meeting of the Society for the Study of Japanese Religions held at the Marriott Hotel, New Orleans; April 12, 1991; p. 13.

[92] Ibid, p.13.

[93] Ibid, p. 14.

52

Because of his Buddhist rhetoric it is quite possible to perceive Nichiren as an individual who is concerned primarily with the propagation of a religious teaching. But do Nichiren's own words clearly and succinctly state that this was his _primary_ purpose? An examination of one of his epistles makes evident that this was not his first and foremost intent. Eight years after the Risshōankokuron was presented (1260), Nichiren wrote a rationale for submitting the Risshōankokuron where he specifically made his intentions clear. As Nichiren wrote:

> I say all this solely for the sake of the nation, for the sake of the Law, and for the sake of others, not for my own sake.[94]

This emphasis that Nichiren placed on the security of the nation was indicative of the depth that Shintō teaching was entrenched in Japanese spirituality. Though it is often dangerous to analyze the psyche of historical religious figures through the comfort of hindsight, it is in Nichiren's bold religious proclamations and political statements that one may conclude that the Shintō religion which places its emphasis on the divinity of the nation (by virtue of its territory being both created by deities as well as inhabited by them) and the divinity of the leaders (the Emperor's lineage to the Sun-goddess), becomes the primary spiritual influence for Nichiren and the primary religious teaching as well: the Buddha-dharma for the security and needs of the nation.

---

[94] The Gosho Translation Committee. ed., trans., The Major Writings of Nichiren Daishonin. Vol. 2, Tokyo: Nichiren Shoshu International Center, 1982, p. 67.

The Shintō teaching that Japan was a nation both divinely created and divinely inhabited strongly influenced Nichiren as to why a nation must strive towards maintaining a balanced and proper relationship with its guardian deities. Nichiren saw his Buddhist teachings as being the means necessary for a troubled nation to restabilize itself. He attempted to convince the government that his form of Buddhism would do just that. Why was he so concerned that if the native kami would "abandon the nation,"[95] this spiritual exodus would result in heretical doctrines that would "create disaster and inflict calamity upon the populace?"[96] Nichiren could have easily ignored the "existence" of the kami and what their presence meant (divine protection for a divinely created nation) and focussed his teachings solely on Buddhism for individual and not national salvation.

Final Conclusion

The uniqueness of Nichiren's teaching compared to the other Buddhist reformers of the Kamakura period lay in his adamant stand on (his) Buddhism as being the way for the nation to right itself. He adhered to the Buddhist teaching of mappō as his doctrinal support for explaining the calamities prevalent in Japan at the time. His concern for the nation stemmed from his

---

[95] Major Writings, Vol. 2, p. 5.

[96] Ibid., p. 5.

Shintō background which taught how the land, the Emperor, and the nation were divinely related.

Nichiren's teaching of Buddhism for the security and prosperity of the nation should be viewed as a Shintō teaching cloaked in Buddhist rhetoric and not as a comfortable fusion of different religious ideologies. His emphasis on protecting the nation through a religious practice was not only a sincere teaching but it was also a means by which Nichiren felt he would gain the necessary economic support from the government for a national propagation.

BIBLIOGRAPHY

Anesaki, Masaharu. *History of Japanese Religion*. London: Kegan Paul, Trench Trubner & Co., Ltd., 1930.

_____. *Religious Life of the Japanese People*. Tokyo: The Society for International Cultural Relations, 1961.

_____. *Nichiren: The Buddhist Prophet*. Gloucester, Mass.: Peter Smith, 1966.

Aston, W.G. *Shintō: The Way of the Gods*. London: Longmans, Green, and Co., 1905.

Baird, Robert D. and Bloom, Alfred. *Indian and Far Eastern Religious Traditions*. New York: Harper & Row, 1972.

Bloom, Alfred. "Shinran" in the *Kodansha Encyclopedia of Japan*. Tokyo: Kodansha International Ltd., 1983.

_____. "Historical Significance of Nichiren's Buddhism." *Young East*, Autumn, 1965.

Collcutt, Martin. *Five Mountains*. Cambridge: Harvard University Press, 1981.

_____. "Eisai" in *The Encyclopedia of Religion*. Mircea Eliade, ed. New York: Macmillan, 1987.

Dobbins, James C. (Oberlin College) "Envisioning Kamakura Buddhism." Paper presented at the Annual Meeting of the Society for the Study of Japanese Religions, April 13, 1991.

de Bary, William Theodore, ed. *The Buddhist Tradition in India, China, and Japan*. New York: Vintage Books, 1969.

Dumoulin, Heinrich. *Zen Buddhism: A History*. Vol. 2. Translated by James W. Heisig and Paul Knitter. New York: Macmillan Publishing Company, 1990.

Earhart, H. Byron. *Japanese Religion: Unity and Diversity*. 3rd. ed. Belmont, California: Wadsworth Publishing Company, 1990.

The Gosho Translation Committee. ed., trans., _The Major_
Writings of Nichiren Daishonin. Vol. 1, Tokyo: Nichiren
Shoshsu International Center, 1979.

_____. ed., trans., _The Major Writings of Nichiren Daishonin_.
Vol. 2, Tokyo: Nichiren Shoshu International Center, 1982.

_____. ed., trans., _The Major Writings of Nichiren Daishonin_
Vol. 3, Tokyo: Nichiren Shoshu International Center, 1985.

_____. ed., trans., _The Major Writings of Nichiren Daishonin_.
Vol. 4, Tokyo: Nichiren Shoshu International Center, 1986.

_____. ed., trans., _The Major Writings of Nichiren Daishonin_
Vol. 5, Tokyo: Nichiren Shoshu International Center, 1988.

_____. ed., trans., _The Major Writings of Nichiren Daishonin_
Vol. 6, Tokyo: Nichiren Shoshu International   Center,
1990.

Grapard, Allan G. "Shintō" in _Kodansha Encyclopedia of_
Japan. Tokyo: Harper and Row, 1983.

Hirai, Naofusa. "Shintō" in _The Encyclopedia of Religion_.
Mircea Eliade, ed. New York: MacMillan, 1987.

Holtom, D.C. _Modern Japan and Shintō Nationalism_. Chicago:
University of Chicago Press, 1943.

Hori, Ichiro. _Folk Religion in Japan_. Edited by Joseph
Kitagawa and Alan L. Miller. Chicago and London:
University of Chicago Press, 1968.

Hurvitz, Leon. trans. _Scripture of the Lotus Blossom of the_
Fine Dharma. New York: Columbia University Press, 1976.

Kato, Genchi. _A Study of Shintō, the Religion of the Japa-_
nese Nation. Tokyo: Meiji Japan Society, 1926.

Kirimura, Yasuji. _Buddhism and the Nichiren Shoshu_
_Tradition._Tokyo: Nichiren Shoshu International Center,
1986.

_____. _Fundamentals of Buddhism_. Santa Monica, World Tribune
Press, 1982.

_____. _The Life of Nichiren Daishonin_. Tokyo: Nichiren
Shoshu International Center, 1980.

Kitagawa, Joseph M. _Religion in Japanese History_. New York:
Columbia University Press, 1966.

Kodera, Takashi James. Dōgen's Formative Years in China.
    Boulder: Prajna Pess, 1980.

Koichi, Shinohara. "Religion and Political Order in Nichiren's
    Buddhism.",Japanese Journal of Religious Studies (Vol.8,
    1981,, Nagoya: Nanzan Institute Religion and Culture).

Mass, Jeffrey P. ed. Court and Bakufu in Kamakura Japan. New
    Haven and London: Yale University Press, 1982.

Matsunaga, Alicia and Daigan. Foundation of Japanese Buddhism.
    Vols. 1,2. Los Angeles: Buddhist Books International, 1976.

Moore, Charles A. ed. The Japanese Mind. Honolulu: University of
    Hawaii Press. 1967.

_____. ed. Philosophy and Culture: East and West. Honolulu:
    University of Hawaii Press, 1968.

Nichiren Daishonin. Kaimoku-Shō. ed.& trans. Kyotsu Hori.
    Tokyo: Nichiren Shu Overseas Propagation Promotion
    Association, 1987.

_____. Senji-Shō. ed.& trans. Kyotsu Hori. Tokyo: Nichiren Shu
    Overseas Propagation Association, 1989.

_____. Hōon-jō. ed. & trans. Taikyo Yajima. Tokyo: Nichiren
    Shu Overseas Propagation Association, 1988.

Philippi, Donald L. trans. Kojiki. Tokyo: University of
    Tokyo Press, 1968.

Rodd, Laurel Rasplica. Nichiren: A Biography. Occasional
    Paper No. 11. Arizona State University, June, 1978.

_____. Nichiren: Selected Writings. Honolulu: The University of
    Hawaii Press, 1980.

Stone, Jackie. "Seeking Enlightenment in the Last Age: Mappō
    Thought in Kamakura Buddhism." Part 1. The Eastern
    Buddhist. Vol.18, nos.1,2, (Spring, Autumn 1985,
    Kyoto: The Eastern Buddhist Society).

_____. (Princeton University) "Reexamining Stereotypes in the
    Study of Nichiren: Nationalism, Intolerance, and
    Independence from Tendai." Paper presented at the
    Annual Meeting of the Society for the Study of
    Japanese Religions, April 12, 1991.

Suzuki, Daisetz Teitaro. Japanese Spirituality. Japan: Japan
    Society for the Promotion of Science, 1972.

Tamura, Kansei. _Nichiren: Risshōankokuron_. Tokyo: Tokuma
     Shoten, 1973.

Tsunetsugu, Muraoka. _Studies in Shintō Thought_. Tokyo:
     Ministry of Education, 1964.

Yokoi, Yuho. _Zen Master Dōgen_. New York: Weatherhill, 1976.

Notes

Printed in the United States
6757

9 781581 121100